I USE MATH/USO LAS MATEMÁTICAS

I USE MATH AT THE STORE/
USO LAS MATEMÁTICAS EN LA TIENDA

Joanne Mattern

Reading consultant/Consultora de lectura: Susan Nations, M.Ed., author/literacy coach/consultant

WR WEEKLY READER
EARLY LEARNING LIBRARY

Please visit our web site at: www.earlyliteracy.cc
For a free color catalog describing Weekly Reader® Early Learning Library's list
of high-quality books, call 1-877-445-5824 (USA) or 1-800-387-3178 (Canada).
Weekly Reader® Early Learning Library's fax: (414) 336-0164.

Library of Congress Cataloging-in-Publication Data available upon request from publisher.
Fax (414) 336-0157 for the attention of the Publishing Records Department.

ISBN 0-8368-6001-2 (lib. bdg.)
ISBN 0-8368-6008-X (softcover)

This edition first published in 2006 by
Weekly Reader® Early Learning Library
A Member of the WRC Media Family of Companies
330 West Olive Street, Suite 100
Milwaukee, WI 53212 USA

Copyright © 2006 by Weekly Reader® Early Learning Library

Managing editor: Valerie J. Weber
Art direction: Tammy West
Cover design and page layout: Dave Kowalski
Photo research: Diane Laska-Swanke
Photographer: Gregg Andersen
Translators: Tatiana Acosta and Guillermo Gutiérrez

Printed in the United States of America

1 2 3 4 5 6 7 8 9 09 08 07 06 05

Note to Educators and Parents

Reading is such an exciting adventure for young children! They are beginning to integrate their oral language skills with written language. To encourage children along the path to early literacy, books must be colorful, engaging, and interesting; they should invite the young reader to explore both the print and the pictures.

I Use Math is a new series designed to help children read about using math in their everyday lives. In each book, young readers will explore a different activity and solve math problems along the way.

Each book is specially designed to support the young reader in the reading process. The familiar topics are appealing to young children and invite them to read and reread again and again. The full-color photographs and enhanced text further support the student during the reading process.

In addition to serving as wonderful picture books in schools, libraries, homes, and other places where children learn to love reading, these books are specifically intended to be read within an instructional guided reading group. This small group setting allows beginning readers to work with a fluent adult model as they make meaning from the text. After children develop fluency with the text and content, the book can be read independently. Children and adults alike will find these books supportive, engaging, and fun!

Nota para los maestros y los padres

¡Leer es una aventura tan emocionante para los niños pequeños! A esta edad están comenzando a integrar su manejo del lenguaje oral con el lenguaje escrito. Para animar a los niños en el camino de la lectura incipiente, los libros deben ser coloridos, estimulantes e interesantes; deben invitar a los jóvenes lectores a explorar la letra impresa y las ilustraciones.

Uso las matemáticas es una nueva colección diseñada para que los niños lean textos sobre el uso de las matemáticas en su vida diaria. En cada libro, los jóvenes lectores explorarán una actividad diferente y resolverán problemas de matemáticas. Cada libro está especialmente diseñado para ayudar a los jóvenes lectores en el proceso de lectura. Los temas familiares llaman la atención de los niños y los invitan a leer y releer una y otra vez. Las fotografías a todo color y el tamaño de la letra ayudan aún más al estudiante en el proceso de lectura.

Además de servir como maravillosos libros ilustrados en escuelas, bibliotecas, hogares y otros lugares donde los niños aprenden a amar la lectura, estos libros han sido especialmente concebidos para ser leídos en un grupo de lectura guiada. Este contexto permite que los lectores incipientes trabajen con un adulto que domina la lectura mientras van determinando el significado del texto. Una vez que los niños dominan el texto y el contenido, el libro puede ser leído de manera independiente. ¡Estos libros les resultarán útiles, estimulantes y divertidos a niños y a adultos por igual!

— Susan Nations, M.Ed., author, literacy coach,
and consultant in literacy development

Mom and I are at the store. We have
a lot to buy!

- - - - - - - - - - - - - - - - -

Mamá y yo estamos en la tienda.
¡Tenemos muchas cosas que comprar!

How many of us are there?

¿Cuántas personas de mi familia vinimos a la tienda?

I put four oranges in a bag.

- - - - - - - - - - - - - - -

Pongo cuatro naranjas en una bolsa.

Oranges cost two for one dollar.
How much will four oranges cost?
- -
Dos naranjas cuestan un dólar.
¿Cuánto costarán cuatro naranjas?

We need a big bag of carrots.
I like to eat them as a snack.

- - - - - - - - - - - - - - - - -

Necesitamos una gran bolsa de
zanahorias. Me gusta comerlas
como tentempié.

If one bag holds eight ounces and one bag holds sixteen ounces, which bag is bigger?

Si una bolsa tiene ocho onzas y otra bolsa tiene dieciséis onzas, ¿qué bolsa es más grande?

We have to buy some meat for dinner.

– – – – – – – – – – – – – – – – –

Tenemos que comprar carne para la cena.

We need six pounds of meat. If each package weighs two pounds, how many packages do we need?

Necesitamos seis libras de carne. Si cada paquete pesa dos libras, ¿cuántos paquetes necesitamos?

I have to find my favorite cereal! It is the third box from the right.

¡Tengo que encontrar mi cereal favorito! Es el de la tercera caja por la derecha.

What color is my favorite box of cereal?

¿De qué color es la caja de mi cereal favorito?

We buy milk and chocolate milk.
I drink lots of milk.

Compramos leche normal y leche
achocolatada. Tomo muchísima leche.

If we buy one carton of white milk and two cartons of chocolate milk, how many cartons do we have?

Si compramos un cartón de leche normal y dos cartones de leche achocolatada, ¿cuántos cartones tenemos?

Now it is time to check out. We wait in line.

Es hora de pagar. Esperamos en la fila.

How many carts are in line in front of us?

¿Cuántos carritos están en la fila antes que el nuestro?

16

Mom lets me give the money to the cashier. Then I give Mom the change.

— — — — — — — — — — — — — — —

Mamá me deja darle el dinero a la cajera. Después le doy el cambio a mamá.

18

Our shopping trip is done. I like helping Mom shop!

– – – – – – – – – – – – – – –

Nuestro viaje a la tienda ha terminado. ¡Me gusta ayudar a mamá con la compra!

How many bags do we have?
¿Cuántas bolsas tenemos?

20

Glossary

cartons — cardboard or plastic containers

cashier — someone who takes money in a store

change — money you get back if you pay too much

ounces — a unit of weight

Glosario

cajero — persona a quien se le paga en una tienda

cambio — dinero que te devuelven si pagas de más

cartones — envases de cartón

onzas — unidad de peso

Answers

Page 4 – 2
Page 6 – $2
Page 8 – 16 ounces
Page 10 – 3
Page 12 – red
Page 14 – 3
Page 16 – 2
Page 18 – $10
Page 20 – 3

Respuestas

Página 4 – 2
Página 6 – $2
Página 8 – 16 onzas
Página 10 – 3
Página 12 – rojo
Página 14 – 3
Página 16 – 2
Página 18 – $10
Página 20 – 3

For More Information/Más información

Books

Let's Visit the Supermarket. Our Community (series).
 Marianne Johnston (PowerKids Press)
Spending Money. Dana Meachen Rau
 (Weekly Reader® Early Learning Library)

Libros

Algo Bueno. Robert Munsch (Annick Press)
De compras con Mamá. Mercer Mayer (Golden Books)

Websites

The Healthy Fridge
www.healthyfridge.org/kids.html
Take the good food quiz to find out about healthy food
choices.

Index

Índice

About the Author

Joanne Mattern is the author of more than 130 books for children. Her favorite subjects are animals, history, sports, and biography. Joanne lives in New York State with her husband, three young daughters, and three crazy cats.

Información sobre la autora

Joanne Mattern ha escrito más de 130 libros para niños. Sus temas favoritos son los animales, la historia, los deportes y las biografías. Joanne vive en el estado de Nueva York con su esposo, sus tres hijas pequeñas y tres gatos juguetones.